Painting the Scene

by

Geoffrey
Wilson

Painting the Scene

© Copyright Geoffrey W. Wilson

First Published by
LUCAS BOOKS 2003

ISBN 1903797-28-4

British Library Cataloguing in Publication Data
A catalogue record for this book is available from the British Library

Printed in the UK by Print Wright Ltd, Ipswich.

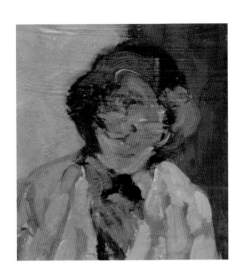

To my Wife

PREFACE

Geoffrey Wilson, Norfolk born and a Chartered Land Agent has set down in the following pages his own experiences, recollections and observations gleaned from a lifetime associated with the land, the countryside and art including at the same time his much enjoyed painting trips abroad. Influenced by Sir Arnesby Brown who lived in the next village, he worked closely for a number of years with the Gorleston based marine artist Rowland Fisher before moving in 1963 to become resident in Lincolnshire. Having continued to exhibit in national and county exhibitions Geoffrey Wilson retired back to Norfolk in January 1983 to paint full-time. He is a Past President of the Lincolnshire Artists' Society.

CONTENTS

Watercolour 7" x 10". On the Amstel, Amsterdam.

Oil 10" x 14". Elixabeth Castle, Jersey.

Chapter One

LAST OF THE LINE

Many of my generation brought up in a large Norfolk village in the 1920s will have memories of the rich pattern of incident that varied the daily routine of childhood. Seasonal activities such as iron hoops and tops had their day, followed as one grew older, by sports in general not forgetting the immense fun of frozen ponds in winter with ice skating and rough ice hockey illumined by the more affluent and older ones amongst us with car headlights. Often of short duration, something to be savoured to the full whilst the "freeze-up" lasted. In the twenties organ grinders complete with monkeys still came round and also the Punch and Judy man. A theatrical touring company made fairly regular appearances with productions of Sweeny Todd, Maria Martin and the Red Barn etc., in a hall attached to one of the public houses. With hindsight, there really was much going on with very active church and chapel life to leaven the interests.

Amateur theatricals started for most with school concerts and I was about six with my first memory in particular still plainly in mind. I cannot recall beyond the fact that I had a line or lines to say at the same time as consuming a bun. Inevitably there were crumbs in evidence and more importantly the audience laughed, which doubtless was the desired intention of the teacher in charge of the production. In this instance, no coaching was necessary, no need to invoke R.A.D.A. The lessons to be learned of projection, control and timing came automatically into play only to be further improved upon and perfected in the next performance.

A few years on in my teens, our Vicar started an amateur dramatic group. He had already made a mark as far as I was concerned by acquiring a splendid painting, probably of Italian origin and having obtained the necessary faculty had it hung on the east end wall of the church above the altar. I believe it is still there. At about the same time to our village came a professional from a West End theatre just closing. Tall, elegant and very sophisticated like the Borzoi dogs he had decided to breed. However, he still yearned for his profession and our Vicar, with great asperity, brought him back into the acting fold. Now this was very different stuff. Expert direction delivered with firmness and authority, but still with grace and reasonable consideration. I recall I had a marvellous part and some great

Watercolour 7" x 10". The Salute Venice (a wet morning).

Oil 12" x 16". Pin Mill, Suffolk.

lines, the humour subtle. A bath was involved with, I think, somebody in it and a great deal hung on the lines in question. The dress rehearsal went fine, and much labour had gone into my coaching. Sadly, at the first performance I made a pig's ear and delivered with an emphasis and inflections that failed and the expected laughter withered on the vine. I hardly recognised our professional never having before witnessed such rage and frustration, or, for myself, experienced such misery. As the reader may well guess, I got it right the next time and thereafter. What joy.

Post war and the amateur theatricals continued mainly in farce with performances in the Public Hall of our nearby market town. Great fun these, including Whitehall Farces. "Almost a Honeymoon", "Will any Gentleman", "See How They Run". A bookmark, annotated, sent me by a member of the audience is a reminder of my role as the Revd. Lionel Toop in the latter and, I believe, how he lost his trousers. The date: 1951. His wife Penelope and husband, long married and with grandchildren, should be lunching with us in a few days time. Our friendship has continued over the years. Natalie Moya, an Adjudicator, praised a performance.

Oil 10" x 12". The Stack Fire, Toft Monks.

I sought a change to an anonymous group of Players produced by a Shakespearean Actor and Producer on an apron stage in Norwich. The play, a tragicomedy, was slated by the critic who said it "neither made you laugh nor cry". Intensely hard work over some weeks with continuous rehearsals, the play defied all efforts by the Producer and cast, including those of the leading lady, a fine professional both on stage and, I believe in radio. The play "Celestina". The playwright, a friend of the Producer, at tea and cakes following his attendance at a matinee performance confided "He would write a better one, just for us"!! My next role was to be in a Passion Play, my part "small, but important". I had to hang on the Cross. This looked like being a draughty assignment and I felt it was becoming imperative for me to decide on another more permanent profession and perhaps to continue with yet another passion, that of brush and canvas. A luminary had come into my purview, very old and nearly blind. I recall him elsewhere in the book.

On looking up artefacts for the forgoing, I turned up a photograph providing a welcome diversion. An organisation had been formed in the County known as Round Table with a branch being established in our local market town. I joined. Young men mainly in sedentary occupations and with heaps of energy jumped at the chance of doing something useful and beneficial in the community and not just meeting a demand to dip a hand in the pocket. A request to a local Lord of the Manor obtained permission for a wilderness adjacent to a rural churchyard to be cleared. The object for Sunday mornings in winter to be spent by members in felling, sawing up, carting, converting to firewood, logs for distribution to needy persons in the market town. This worked well and enthusiasm knew no bounds. School Teachers, Bank Staff, a Bus Operator (handy as the town was six miles from the site) an oil company manager, builders, Insurance staff, shopkeepers, a

Oil 10" x 12". The Scissor Grinder (last of the line).

jolly crowd with much to contribute. All provided tools, some with the facility, more than others. Voluntary help came with a tractor and trailer and, I believe a truck from a member. Memory fades, but I feel sure it carried on for more than one year. The need was great, probably still is. However, difficult today, perhaps, to find working fireplaces. In many instances, impossible to find a chimney!! The end result, a bit of comfort, a wilderness cleared and a rabbit warren eradicated. Even the neighbours must have been pleased.

Services came to the street and the door.

Oil 12" x 15". Reedham Ferry, Winter.

It was in 1951, another much smaller village, married and with a family, that I painted a small panel – my earliest extant picture – of a scissor grinder. He called very early in the morning and we availed ourselves of his services and he sharpened up all our cutting tools. Our eldest, a daughter about five was intrigued to stand and watch the Scissor Grinder at his tasks all regulated by the deft use of his foot pedal. He never came again. It was his final call and future sharpenings required a visit to the nearest town and, I think, a tinsmith to do the job. It was only a short question of time before he too disappeared from the scene.

Chapter Two

THOUGHTS ON ART IN GENERAL AND PAINTING IN PARTICULAR

How does the embryo painter sort it all out? What a maze of methods and techniques present themselves for the student to select a best way to express that creative urge. Inevitably there must be the desire to draw. A sobering thought, of course, the held belief that a draughtsman of quality is born and not bred – that it is true so many can be trained to become adequate, but only a very few will ever achieve a sublime line and exquisite drawing. However, the ultimate goal applies to all things in all walks in life.

A method which appeals must be decided upon – by line with or without various processes and mediums, the camera itself perhaps, or the more familiar mediums of water colour pure and simple and not so simple, chalks, pastels, oil paint dilute, loaded in heavy impasto – perhaps a mix, the more recent acrylic and doubtless the student will work in most methods and finally settle for a few. Oh to be a J.M.W. Turner and use all or any at will and still get to the heart of the matter.

Reading and research will be a large part of the process together with a multitude of disciplines to be observed, learned and not forgotten. Of course, one could go in hell-bent with a by-guess and by-God approach, buttressed by an insane conviction of a "calling" and that genius will out!! An expensive and short lived aberration if nothing else. Somewhere along the line may be the struggle over what is figurative and representational and what is abstract in all its various guises. Perhaps a cross between the two can be embraced. The figurative pursuit raises the spectre of an "illustrator", or will the student seek a method of greater depth without falling between two stools.

Anyway, not for him to worry whether John Crome in writing meant breath as opposed to breadth. Doubtless his intention was one and the same anyway. R.H. Wilensky may well have had a point when he wrote of "the cherry to be pecked at"* approach as one in which there can be no future. One reads that Chardin had the answers as did all the great and the immortals. From whence the source, be it from nature, images of the mind, or whatever the means, complex or simple, can only serve to an end, which should be a concept honed as fine as the artist can make it.

*From "English Painting" by R. H. Wilensky, Faber & Faber Ltd.

At the Royal Scottish Academy:

Comment by a painter of great bravura on a picture in which a hedge went right across it: "[He] waved his hand in a great circle and said 'Knock a hole in the hedge and let in the Absolute'. We all knew what he meant and he was right!" (Letters to the author from Stanley Cursiter, CBE, RSA, 31.9.1970 (sic) and 19.10.1970)

The painter that Stanley Cursiter referred to was Peter Wishart, an Associate of the R.S.A., and I quote again from his letter "...rugged and hirsute, but he always wore a bowler hat and a green leaf in his buttonhole, even if only a leaf of privet off his hedge...he was an erratic and spontaneous painter – determined to capture the effect he saw in the quickest manner – sunlight, atmosphere, wind were his ideals – and this he did in a very personal way – but always distinguished by fine quality of colour".

The author personally recalls a large shoreline picture by Peter Wishart of boys bathing, a glorious sky and sea, all executed as described in the letter extract above and with it in mind led him to purchase at auction a work by this artist. It was a river scene also executed with great bravura, enlivened by an angler, the figure blended in beyond compare in a superbly handled composition. The work bore a label "The Artists Haunt", a puzzle for the author, but not for his correspondent and I quote again from Stanley Cursiter's letters: "The title of his picture might well be confused by his penmanship – if I remember aright he used a quill pen which he cut himself! – I remember he sent a picture to the RSA – it was the interior of a

Oil 12" x 16". Bright Pastures, Haddiscoe.

cowshed, but had a hen running across the foreground. It appeared in the catalogue as "In terror" and people wondered what had frightened the hen – all that Peter had written was "Interior". From this it seemed reasonable to conclude that the title of the picture the author had purchased was really "The Anglers Haunt" and not the "Artists". What lessons there are to be learned. How to keep one's feet on the ground and to look and see more clearly! A fine artist looking at one of my paintings observed "A nice simple composition". Some time later I realised I had been paid a compliment and one doesn't have to go down the road of "minimalism" to achieve simplicity. Clarity, surely, in all things and if you cannot "read it" go back to view and think again. Tags on styles may well seem reckless when the novelty wears off and the fact that it hasn't been seen before is not sufficient to justify a new school in perpetuity. A layer of brick in pattern, or even an unmade bed does not necessarily point to a new lead in artistic activity even if temporarily capable of arousing a furore and cultural fever in the eyes and minds of the beholders.

AT AUCTION

I recall the painter Arnesby Brown telling me how much he preferred painting trees in winter with branches bare of leaves and with the skeleton plainly visible. I can only remember seeing one of his pictures in this vernacular, a medium sized

Oil 12" x 16". Bungay From The Beccles Road (an April day).

oil, at auction and quite an early work. Market forces may have something to do with a scarcity and perhaps it is that summertime has a greater general appeal in the mind's eye than winter. The composition was dominated by a huge tree, short boled with an enormous top, superbly seen and painted. I put in a bid without success. In fact, I have put in a bid without success for an Arnesby Brown picture on several occasions.

One of these was for an oil that had lived in Canada, about 14" x 18" canvas size of cattle coming up the Carr Farm marsh drift at Norton Subcourse, in high summer with the atmosphere impregnated with dust and heat all superbly expressed by this great artist in a small canvas. A reader may recall a similar work by him with cattle storming over the old lift bridge on Haddiscoe Cut. I only saw it once and the picture left me with an indelible impression. To get back to the Norton scene, it was View Day, we were shortly off on holiday, the year 1972 and as usual I left my bid. Walking back, I missed my wife who had returned to the auctioneer's office and knowing how much I was taken by the work, had increased my bid to an amount double the sale room estimate. In fairness, I would point out that this was not "home territory" for Arnesby Browns (although it should have been) and the estimate to my mind was modest. Just as well for the forthcoming holiday perhaps, I was yet again unsuccessful. Someone, somewhere was possibly cornering the market.

For a painter, collecting pictures can be a two-edged sword. A fiscal justification may be invoked as a hedge against inflation! The painter's knowledge

Oil 10" x 12". Landscape, Red House Farm (where the Skylarks sing).

on art may well be of help in spotting not only a worthwhile work, but also a good investment. Conversely, a judgement influenced by the direction of his own painterly inclinations can easily cloud his perceptions on subject matter and market trends.

On one aspect I think a certainty can prevail – be prepared to consider going the extra mile. Not confined to art, living with a desired acquisition surely must be sweeter than having to bemoan its loss.

Chapter Three

OUR BIRDS

We live in a house in the middle of a meadow, falling to a marshy area through which runs a rivulet fed by springs and in no time reaches the "Beck" in turn gravitating more slowly through the village, across the marshes to discharge by gravitation, or pump into the main river.

I say "Our birds" because, having withstood the perils of modern agricultural practice, now modified if only just, there appears to be a considerable resurgence in some species and perhaps the milder winters have helped. The house is old and the house sparrow that virtually disappeared from our roofs have multiplied. The parents urge their offspring from beneath the tiles on to the edge of the gutter and with varying degrees of impatience make the fledglings take a first flight hopefully not beyond our boundary. Further on are numerous hazards not least of which are marauding cats. The return of bats swooping and diving in the gloaming bring to mind advice at one time common in the countryside for ladies to cover their heads to avoid entanglement with "high divers". The great joy of the song thrush is again in evidence with occasionally the much larger missel thrush amongst them. The blue tits for years bringing off their brood in the casing of our pump no longer used. This effort with variable success as sometimes the fledglings wouldn't make it through the aperture at the top of the pump handle (tied town to try and ensure the main chance) and one great disaster when it was found that the nest complete with babies had fallen from its precarious perch at the head of the pump right down to the bottom at ground level. All dead.

An ancient apple tree once described to me as "a kind of codling" bears lots of fruit that ripens in early August and is thus normally the prey for wasps, but not this year, 2000. Also, the forceful depredations of blackbirds, a greater host than ever and which for the first time has denied our efforts to harvest a sufficiency for the filling of apple pies as no better flavour can be found. The blackbirds have completely ruled the roost, pecking at the fruit until it has fallen to the ground and even feeding any offspring dilatory in survival techniques, feasting not only on new falls, but also any rotten bits of apple that come to hand. Do I notice a slight "stagger" in the hopping gait of older birds? Cider with Rosie comes to mind as I sip my morning cup and gaze at the scene outside the window.

So independent and appearing not to be afraid of anything, the two territorial robins (one from the East and one from the West end of the garden) move about and enjoy a "peck" as the fancy takes them.

By comparison, our local barn owl who really is well situated for the richest of pickings seems to make hard work of finding something to eat. Anyway, he flaps his way around the property, and stands on a fence post from time to time in apparent contemplation. I think he must be lazy, or have an increasing family problem, otherwise why bother to be active during the day as well as in the evening? I should say "they" because its Mr and Mrs, without a doubt. We know where they live and its quite inaccessible thank goodness.

Finches and wagtails add colour to the scene and occasionally a starling, so recently in abundance, roosting en masse in young woodlands, but which now appear to have left the countryside for the towns.

The forgoing was written last summer in the year 2000. Now it is spring again in the year 2001, following the wettest autumn and winter we have experienced for many years. The house and garden is on sand. To the south between the garden and the rivulet the marshy peat soil has foot drains at intervals discharging into the stream. One of the foot drains has expanded into a small pond and provides the refuge for a pair of wild duck. The remainder of the meadow is a former sandpit from ancient times, the area known as "The Links". The marshy bit is always green. The rest, including our garden, requires a good rain every week and rarely gets it in normal times. In the summer, three weeks without a rain and the area has overtones of Provence without the rocks! Snipe continue to inhabit the rivulet where it widens into a stream. No change in "Our

Oil 12" x 16". Low Meadows, Mettingham.

Birds" that I have noted to date. The barn owls continue with their peregrinations. The missel thrush sits authoritatively looking outwards through the orange twigs of the weeping willow. By outwards I mean beyond our boundary. The song thrush, the blackbirds, house sparrows, blue tits, black caps, bull finches etc., dart hither and thither between short perches on the post and rail fencing surrounding the property. The robins maintain their territory east and west.

Despite global warming we are very much in a frost pocket. After at least twelve years since planting, the magnolia has at last reached 5' 6" and looks well. Thank goodness I have so far resisted all attempts to make me lift it and replant somewhere else. The second week of April and full of blossom in bud – I hope I do not have to eat my words! Again no serious frosts this winter – two or three inches of snow came and went in a trice and I managed a water colour from the draining board looking across to the Hall Farm, between sips of morning tea. The blue tits have been going in and out of the pump handle entrance to the "casing" like crazy. Our big worry, there is no "Sophie". The marauding cats from time to time encircle the perimeter rabbit fence. One cheekily came down the drive to the gate, then casually strolled back with leisurely glances around as though to say "Who cares". A male blackbird sits with a beady eye for ages, again looking out beyond our boundary from his perch at the top of a young pollarded lime. He may well be keeping watch. Every year there is at least one nest in the Kolkwitzia bush to his left. We seldom put out water now, the frosts are slight. The habitat provides an excellent diet and I cut the short grass surrounding the house throughout the winter. This suits our birds and a lot more besides. A rich mix with the tussocky variety around and the marshy flora just beyond. The last week in April and our song thrush has no tail!! He has plainly had a lucky escape and we do not fancy his chances. Sophie must be turning in her grave.

THE SKYLARK (A VIGNETTE)

One of those early summer Sunday mornings, the kind of day when it is difficult to contemplate anything more sublime we, my friend George and I had motored along the New Dam and set up our easels in the middle of the marsh. The cattle were static and dozing from the warm sun and the air was vibrant with the singing of skylarks hovering on high, some having first descended in a twitter to nearer the level to check our intrusion. Noting we too were still, all was full again with the sounds of nature. The monotony of a pile driver out to the North West at Reedham having either exhausted itself, or its operators, meant the skylarks reigned supreme.

Later, assembled in Rowland's studio we assessed our recent work including the morning's efforts. When my turn came, Rowland mused awhile and briefly all was silent and then, in a very soft voice and pointing to the middle distance of my morning's endeavour he spoke "And Geoffrey, that is where the skylarks sing". He was a wise man.

Not anymore Rowland, I fear these have now long gone.

Chapter Four

COINCIDENCE (One and Two)

One Sunday evening in 1956 I was working in the confines of my friend and mentor's "lookout" at the top of his house – completely at the top as it was a projection above the house roof and accessed only by a companionway ladder and then a trapdoor in the lookout floor. He was drawing and I was painting a small panel of the harbour entrance still with its "pagoda" like structure and, in the foreground, the "storm house" replete with slatted lookout. My friend casually enquired "Anything to view?", referring to the large and splendid brass telescope already trained out to sea. I obliged, looked and then looked again before replying to the effect that some miles out and almost hull down was a huge aircraft carrier thrashing along at top speed and partly obscured by plumes of spray. With colliers from the North still his most frequent viewing, my friend gave a dry and slightly disbelieving chuckle and took over. "By God you're right" he said. He kept the vessel in sight for as long as he could traverse the telescope. The next morning I read that the aircraft carrier "Ark Royal" had left Scapa Flow to join the fleet assembled for the Suez conflict in which we had teamed up with the French against Nasser and the Egyptians, losing our standing for the time being with the Americans. What history has made of it all has as yet, I suppose, to be fully evaluated.

COINCIDENCE TWO

Some seventy years ago my friend Wesley and I were being taken to Norwich in his father's car to get a haircut. This had latterly been the arrangement as at the time the village didn't have a barber's shop. I think it was autumn, not spring and already dusk. The seating in the car was spacious, the three of us in the front seat, Wesley next to his father and myself sitting on the near side.

About six miles along the road on the curving brow of the steepest hill in the district we were suddenly confronted by a stationary lorry of the type to carry ballast, or similar. No room to pass, no time, no time, a jamming on of brakes the violent turning of an avoiding wheel, the crash of impact and the scrunch of

Oil 14" x 11". Autumn Roses. (ROI Autumn Exh. 1966. Cat. No 44.)

rending metal. Wesley's father no longer in the car. Careering up the bank on my side and down the steep decline a figure walking loomed large in front of us and disappeared. Still further down the hill and into the opposite bank at a perilous angle, Wesley, with great presence of mind, leaned over, pulled hard on the hand brake and we stopped. All over, neither of us hurt.

In those days an accident on the highway was relatively rare, a fatality rarer still and a double fatality almost unheard of. Two men dead, both of the same name, but unrelated, two wives widowed likewise and several children made fatherless.

I move on to the late sixties, perhaps the early seventies. A Royal Norfolk Show Dinner for the Judges, four or six at table. An elderly man was leading a conversation and to my astonishment the story above unfolded. Comments were made and turning to me the speaker repeated, "Yes, two small boys, both unhurt". "I know" I said, "I was one of them".

Chapter Five

RANDOM THOUGHTS

Wherein lies the soul. What is it elevating one's consciousness to that which seems to be an altogether higher plane. Music generally expressed as the highest of the Arts and as a catalyst doubtless plays its part on the emotions. I recall when walking in through the great west door of the cathedral at Chartres to being virtually stunned by the thunderous blast of an organ voluntary that excluded all other sensations and, dare I say it, seemed to transport the soul. It turned out to be the funeral service for a local rugby hero who had died tragically a few days earlier.

On another occasion when staying in Dieppe we went to Varengeville up the road to look at the church, admire Bracque's marvellous window and to see his marble tomb outside. My time to paint and with help from my wife we carried the gear walking East a measured (looking back) distance and just beyond a shallow ravine I set up my easel and got to work. Yet again I became conscious of an elation which I can only describe as being a kind of lifting of the spirit. Anyway, it was a joyous feeling and the work went well. Some years later at a Monet exhibition in London I stood and saw for the first time his picture of Varengeville Church and in the immediate foreground, just East of the shallow ravine, the spot from whence it was painted. I have wondered since, had efforts gone worse than usual, would I have sounded off as a doubting Thomas!

We were staying in Tellaro redolent of Shelley and years before I had heard of Porto Fino and had seen that delightful film "Enchanted April". Here was a place to paint and just beyond our "villa" by steps descending to a narrow road running at right angles down a steep decline, let into a niche in the rocks was a Pardon with a sculpted image of the Virgin and Child, the domed recess painted a celestial blue and in front and just below the figures a wondrous posy of flowers. People, nearly all women and nearly all in black came intermittently down the street, not all old by any means, many much younger than I, paused, made the sign of the cross, bowed and murmured "Mama Mia". Many looked and smiled as I worked and I felt I was in a good place.

On a more pragmatic plane, my mind goes back to a few days painting in Kent. Early September, cloudless skies supposedly, scorching heat and the

Oil 12" x 10". Roadside Shrine, Tellaro ("A wondrous posy of flowers").

Oil 10" x 12". Eglise de Varenge Ville ("A lifting of the spirit").

Oil 10" x 12". Ebbtide, Gorleston. (ROI Autumn Exh. 1978. Cat. No 384.)

unbridled burning of straw, from the corn harvest rapidly nearing completion. Each and every day the sun seen as a dull golden orb in a smoke filled sky of varying degrees of opacity. Even along the coast we hardly saw the sea, our throats rasping from the acrid fumes transmitted by this pernicious habit. And, of course, it wasn't just the straw. Trees here and there showing up as flaming torches, road verges frizzled and where there had been road improvements and the provision of impregnated post and rail fences these sometimes well alight and blazing away to ash and charred remains. The thought crossed my mind how could this possibly fit in with the medical profession's exhortations to avoid passive smoking? At least I suppose the Fire Service must have benefited from unremitting practice.

Wearing my other hat I had to contend with the problem, so intractable as are all such problems when tied to economics. Good relations and being "on the spot" helped. N.F.U. Codes of conduct getting firmer each year gradually played their part and eventually, of course, there was legislation. However, in my purview salvation appeared in the form of a factory ideally situated which utilised straw as a matrix for its finished product – a feeding stuff I believe and not a ceiling board. The price paid for the straw just marginally covering the cost of baling, carting and delivering over three or four miles.

Anyway, I suppose if it is not one thing its another. "Set aside" seems to produce some extraordinary autumn tints here and there at odd times of the year!!

Some will be familiar with the dictum of the nineteenth century French painter, Thomas Couture, on a work of immediacy, done directly from the subject as "Having a logic of spontaneity to which reasoning can add nothing". Generally expressed in French as an "Etude" and in English with the all embracing term "sketch". Anyway, how can one describe it? Perhaps as a kind of shorthand in painting, not only in the drafting and execution, but also in the feeling (colour and tone), uncluttered by detail, the very essence of the subject portrayed. On viewing, a jolt for the beholder into an acceptance of a vision untrammelled, hopefully an Arcadian delight. None ever more successful in this regard than the painter from Flatford. A Constable sketch with its immediate quickening of the senses has just that effect. The question of finish plagues all painters. I have heard it referred to as "the dead hand", not that it has to be dead, but occuring sufficiently often to invoke yet another saying: "Two men to paint a picture, one to paint and the other to tell him when to stop"! The creative muse is sensitive indeed and may have long departed whilst the brush wielding arm labours on.

Chapter Six

NO MAN IS AN ISLAND

This book gives me the chance to mention at least some of the artists whose friendship, or acquaintance I have enjoyed over the years.

Sir John Arnesby Brown who sadly I only got to know in the early 1950s when for some time he had partly lost his sight, in his eighties, was to me a dignified and private figure. I see him now, kneeling in his front hall to peer closely at my humble efforts. How I wished, each time on leaving, I could have produced something better for him to look at. Words of wisdom:-

On subject matter: "Be diligent in your selection as to whether it will, in fact, lend itself to pictorial interpretation." A bit of advice endorsed years later in a letter from Anna Airy.

On composition: "Always subordinate in the picture everything to that you wish to portray."

On my last visit to him he gave me his little Robersons sketch box, with the long-dried palette still laid out. In all my years of painting I have scarcely ever varied from it. The lid of the box, in the grooves, takes very thin panels (perhaps cigar box lids or similar), precisely 8 ¾" x 10 ¹¹/₁₆". At the auction after his death I was told his large studio easel plus a roll of wire netting went for ten shillings!

My friend, farmer and painter George Cargill had inherited a fine painting talent from his mother. We first met whilst labouring with tractors, Land Rovers and sandbags to try and stop the 1953 floods extending beyond Boyce's Dyke at Norton to the Low Road. The wind got up, for us, from the wrong quarter and we didn't succeed.

For years we attended every R.A. Summer Exhibition, going through it with a "fine-tooth comb". Our wives also went through – at speed – then off shopping, back for lunch, and the four of us for further viewing and contemplation. George's wonderful sense of humour knew no bounds. Lowry's men (not the "stick" variety) with huge and shiny toe caps to their "high-lows" (boots) and Ruskin Spear's "Lady with a strawberry mousse" are subjects that come to mind for merriment and landscapes by Reginald Brundrit and R.O. Dunlop et al we found thrilling. A "speedy" ride home and a "jar" at Blythburgh White Hart would conclude a near perfect day. For this man, his love of nature and sheer exuberance in being out

Oil 12" x 16". Winter Landscape, Ashby.

Oil 20" x 24". Back Street, Gorleston. (ROI Autumn Exh. 1979. Cat. No 394.)

and about made him a most delightful companion. May I invite the reader to imagine a brilliant summer day, the Aldeburgh Carnival and dancing in procession behind the silver band to "Lily the Pink". One could go on. Good songs in those days. The Banana Boat Song comes to mind. George died young leaving a widow and four lovely daughters.

We joined the Great Yarmouth Society of Artists, together with George Roberts, a friend who a few years later held a number of successful exhibitions in Norwich. The Chairman of the Society, soon to become its President, Rowland Fisher and his wife Rebecca became friends and I worked extensively with him between 1956 and 1962. Rowland exhibited widely in national exhibitions in the Capital and encouraged me to do the same. A strong swimmer and, he told me, a one time wrestler, also a tennis player, I little thought as a boy on holiday one of the two men swimming between the piers at Great Yarmouth and watched by crowds would play quite an important part in my artistic endeavours.

Also a member of the Norfolk and Norwich Art Circle it was there I first met that paragon of women artists Anna Airy. She was opening the annual exhibition at the Castle Museum. I had wandered off elsewhere in the building when a command came over the tannoy for me to meet her to discuss a work of mine. We met and thereafter met again on several occasions and also corresponded until shortly before her death in 1964. What a wonderful turn of phrase she had. In writing of Lincolnshire (we had moved there in February 1963) and having opened the Lincolnshire Artists' annual exhibition at the Usher Gallery, Lincoln, some

Oil 12" x 16". Marshside Market Garden, Haddiscoe.

years earlier, she described that vast rolling landscape with the stricture "...and Scunthorpe looks the other way".* (But Anna, what a 'Bedlam Furnace!!!). I admired her enormously.

The Lincolnshire Artists' Society and the Usher Gallery became the centre of my artistic activity. Stanley Barrell, at least twice Chairman, an architect member, painter and etcher became a friend. We had, with our wives a painting trip touring France and, after retirement yet another at La Rochelle. It was a splendid venue. A raconteur with the driest of wits Stanley was a wonderful companion. At selection for the Usher Exhibition he looked down on a picture from his lofty perch (he was a tall man) and I heard him murmur "A bit of soft porn I see!").

Max Marschner and Norfolk-born wife Jill have long been friends. Both are artists of great talent and Max, a printmaker, lecturer and a past Chairman has set up his presses in a business at home. Together with an equally talented family they have for many years added prestige to the Society's exhibitions.

Paul Haigh, a retired G.P. had sold his boat after extensive travels. He and his wife became friends. We painted together and met regularly and had a mutual friend in Gill Nadin who, having trained at the Bath Academy under Scott and Armitage moved home to Lincolnshire and became a leading light in the "Society". A stunning painter, etcher and unreservedly praised as an inspirational teacher Gill had a very considerable impact on the artistic life in the County. We each served as Chairman twice, extending over several years, and Gill held office in other capacities as well. She enjoyed visits here after our return to Norfolk in January 1983. More recently, when staying with a niece in London over Christmas Gill suffered a stroke from which she failed to recover. A visit here after Christmas had been planned. Her loss to Lincolnshire's Artistic community was immense.

---

* Letter to the author, 7th May, 1964

Chapter Seven

THE HURRICANE

Painting from Poole Quay a prospect across the harbour to Sandbanks on the morning of Friday, October 16th 1987, my mind went back to a not altogether different kind of day years previously when staying with my family at the Old Ferry Inn, Bodinnick on the Fowey estuary – shades of Daphne Du Maurier's "Frenchman's Creek". It was early afternoon with a stifling atmosphere as I worked on my painting looking along the estuary and out to sea. The depression deepened and all before me seemed to become one in a dense dark sulphurous envelope. I could barely see to work – all verging on the cataclysmic.

A pleasure boat came up from Falmouth loaded with passengers, moored and disembarked at Fowey. They may have had tea. In the meantime the depression deepened further and the sea became increasingly in turmoil. Consideration may possibly have been given to defer, or not to return by sea. However, the passengers re-embarked and the vessel sailed off into the incredible gloom and mounting waves. On its way, possibly near Black Head, Chapel Point, or Dodman Point the vessel, overwhelmed, foundered in the raging storm with all on board.

This day in October 1987 was not altogether dissimilar in the unreal and eerie conditions that prevailed. The atmosphere not sulphurous, but livid, an uneasy calm and an unruffled surface to the water of the bay prevailed. That night was the night of the great hurricane with winds up to and in excess of one hundred miles per hour. Millions left with no electricity, roofs stripped, copings collapsed and huge pines felled in their hundreds criss-crossing the Bournemouth chines. The devastation was immense. The Storm had travelled across the country in a North Easterly direction and on our return journey to Norfolk further damage was evident, but as nothing compared with what met our eyes near home. The great oak, many so carefully preserved in hedgerows, clumps and spinneys, if not uprooted, thrust torn and mangled stumps of branches to the sky. The splendid elms had disappeared through Elm disease and the beech in the area already decimated by virtue of age and, an inadequate rainfall. Now, it seems, it was the turn of the oak. Nature will have its way.

Oil 10" x 12". Tail-End of a Hurricane, Penzance.

Chapter Eight

BOUNDARIES AND DRAINS

I once enquired from a friend of mine whose relative had been a great collector, whether that was his prime interest. Good heavens no, came the reply, drains and boundaries. On reflection, this leavening is what life is all about. Too rarefied and specialist full time pursuits may become irksome. No one more narrow minded than the professional may well become the cry. Prosaic interests in fundamental and practical matters can be a foil and make for a balance between two extremes. Acknowledging that in the final assessment, legal expertise must prevail in these matters, it is the wide ranging, local and common sense aspects that will unravel most of the problems. Boundaries in dispute, with frequently so many ambivalent possibilities, time span and common usage views to contend with must be stressful and in the long term costly to resolve. Boundaries defined by the ubiquitous Leylandii are perhaps the modern "marker" to bring more grief than benefit. Partly, I suspect due to present day attitudes prevailing with a "quick fix" on the one hand and a failure on the other to appreciate, or accept, the greater burden of control and responsibility over maintenance – an intemperate habit of growth in a temperate clime!!

Drains, of course, may well incorporate boundaries in themselves. The term "Levels" can embrace whole counties with even wider implications. To start at the other end – gulleys and footdrains – how we miss the highways lengthmen of years gone by! Land drains with out-falls into ditches. Many "schemes" have got underway in modern times only to discover when work commences that in the 19th century "golden age" it had all been done before with "outfalls" still operating once the secondary system of ditches met the required depth. Foot drains, sock dykes (one ended), dykes gravity operated or pumped, becks as distinct from small streams spring fed wending their way to a main river and on to tidal reaches. Costing us all "a bomb" even if we don't realise we are paying to keep them moving and are for our mutual well being. Finally, the "Septic Tank". No man worth his salt would, of course, be without his "set of rods".

A combination of tides, gales and rain gave rise to the great flood disaster of 1953 affecting nearly all the eastern seaboard of the country resulting in great loss of life, damage and loss of property and inundation by salt water. Sea and river walls were breached and so on down the scale to relatively small rivers and dykes when strong offshore winds piled high the salt water of incoming tides, topped sandbagged defences and flooded marsh areas far inland. When the waters receded, restoration took time with applications of gypsum to reduce the salinity and copious quantities of lime, and basic slag, with the addition of fertilisers to bring back a balance of nutrients essential for good grass and also arable cropping where appropriate if the land was to be brought into full agricultural production. The repair of breached sea walls was a massive undertaking and to an extent is still ongoing.

After some years, with a degree of normality returning, yet another problem appeared. Introduced into this country years previously for its fur (nutria) the coypu, a large South American rodent weighing up to 25lbs or more and originally kept under control conditions, escaped and the marshy tracts of East Anglia largely deserted for six months of the year seemed to provide a perfect habitat for these creatures resulting in our river and dyke banks being destabilised by holes and burrows making them more like colanders than barriers. Our area between the rivers Yare, Waveney and Chet affecting broads, marshes and low lying land quickly became heavily infested. The coypu appeared to have no natural enemies and a suggestion that it might make a useful contribution to the food chain (coypu cutlets!) found no takers. The already established local rabbit clearance societies took the initial move to at least try and contain the invasion. The press helped by visiting and photographing affected river banks and the image of these

Oil 10" x 12". A Spring Day, St. Olaves.

huge rats breaking through the land surface of walls and banks, highlighted the seriousness of the situation. Publicity was also given on television and radio programmes. Trapping and shooting was successful, but it took a long time to make an impression. Fortunately, there were no inundations in the interim to worsen the problem. Eventually eradication was mounted on a national scale and it took several years for the "last" coypu to be cleared. Control of rabbits, always a great bone of contention when infesting boundaries, became academic with the advent of that dreadful flea borne disease, myxomatosis.

Chapter Nine

HOME AND FAMILY

I was born late in my parents' lives, my mother a fortnight short of her 49th birthday – quite a shock I would imagine and, I suppose, relatively rare in 1920. My father, five and a half years older than my mother was born in 1865, my mother in 1871. She apparently had trouble carrying a child when younger and suffered a number of miscarriages. Her doctor, with a wisdom, advised she could be more successful when older. The result was first an adopted daughter. Later, a son who survived for ten years in a spinal carriage (the outcome of an instrumental birth) and who promptly died when deprived of my mother's nursing care on the advent of my elder brother, some five years prior to my arrival. Instrumental help doubtless saved many lives, but not all. A friend with his jocular, twisted smile and deafness on one side was living proof of a "survival".

Very much in mind with the new Norfolk and Norwich University Hospital now "on stream" are historical facts in our local paper appertaining to the present edifice, and the great things that transpired in the 1880s including the work and munificence of the surgeon, Mr.Cadge.

The 30th December 1882 found my father at 17 practising with an old pistol, his intention to join the army. The pistol exploded taking half his left hand with it. My memory is of just the index finger and thumb remaining. He was conveyed in the back of a horse-drawn cart the twelve or so miles to the Norfolk and Norwich, one might perhaps assume rather more dead than alive. This has prompted us to visit the Record Office to check in the appropriate Register at the time. I quote:-

Date of Accident	....	30.12.82
Date of Admission	....	30.12.82
Date of Operation	....	30.12.82
Accident	....	Gunshot wound of the hand
Operation	....	Partial Amputation
Date of Recovery	....	17th March 1883
The Surgeon	....	Mr. H.S.Williams

From the forgoing it is plain to understand why the Norfolk and Norwich has for so long had such a great reputation. The ten weeks stay seems long. No evidence to support the family story however that my father succumbed to "lockjaw" (tetanus) and was the first to survive there with this, invariably at that time, fatal condition.

Each page of the Register something of a revelation! Kidney stones a scourge and seldom more than two deaths per page of admissions. My father collected for the hospital, as did hundreds of others, each year throughout my memory. It was a great day in our village of Hempnall, the cricket meadow full of people, the brass band and a combined church Service. All the Friendly Societies represented with banners, their officers with brilliantly coloured sashes (I still have my father's) and other regalia, bearing the heavily laden "hospital" boxes, the results of touring the parishes weeks beforehand collecting donations in their spare time. Not that there was much of that, the 40 hour week was still a long way off!!

My father died in 1935. My mother in 1959 in her 89th year. Coming from a large family she would recall her experience riding "pillion" on a "boneshaker", a precursor of the bicycle. I am nor sure about a saddle, or pedals, but as they lived in Tasburgh near the school and at the top of a steep hill they had the impetus for at least a short trip!

Oil 12" x 15". A Willing Horse (The Wilson children).

She was a voracious reader and correspondent and I recall, when she was in her eighties and living with us, the numerous letters she exchanged with a retired farmer in the Fens over an apple with the evocative name of "Sopsy Wine". A correspondence so extensive it seemed that a romance could be blossoming! An appearance on a radio programme really got her going and she fed the writer J.Wentworth Day from time to time with titbits for his articles in "Country Life".

Visitors to our home at Hempnall were quite numerous, mostly from my paternal side as many had moved to London and doubtless yearned for a breath of country air. Aunt Lizzie Read comes top of my list. Aesthetic features, a parchment skin, thick lensed spectacles, in appearance the embodiment of satin and lace with button-up boots and a very pronounced lisp which went splendidly with her London (not cockney) accent. She kept a corner shop selling confectionery etc., somewhere in Notting Hill and always came to us well supplied from "stock". Her husband, my Uncle Bob had lost an eye which, with his beard, gave him a rather fierce look. He also had the disconcerting habit of, on occasions, appearing with the "glass" one missing. Actually, I think my brother and I were a bit scared of him, probably not without reason as we could both be trying and he had rather "a short fuse". A Read cousin Lila sang with the Carl Rosa Opera Company and a Scandrett offshoot, Frank, managed the art shop of Lechertier Barbe in Jermyn Street. As I recall it, just to go into this establishment was an "artistic tonic" in itself. "Goose quills", "Venice turps", a "kit kat canvas", I was sure here were the real artists. Nearly all in black, the accoutrements larger than life – broad-brimmed hats, cloaks, stovepipe trousers and a fund of knowledge expressed with an expertise and in terms I found difficult to follow. Cousin Frank was a painter and, I fancy, nearly last of the line of managers as, following his retirement, it was not so many years before the shop ceased to exist. Aunt Polly, my father's sister lived in Wimbledon. I think her husband had died, her two sons Reggie and Harold quite grown up. The former was an ardent motor cyclist who spent most weekends in trips to Brooklands which was in its motor racing heyday. Eventually, on a return journey, Cousin Reggie had an accident and lost a leg. However, a good artificial replacement ensured he could continue to follow his Brooklands passion. All long ago and becoming "shadowy" with time!

Even more shadowy, a photograph from abroad and now lost – a rarity, I would add, as I am a great hoarder – of a dominant central figure clad in tropical attire with a rifle across his knees and the name Kendal comes to mind. On either side staff similarly clad with a number of natives around and beyond. Is it my fancy, or was I told he was the Superintendent to the building of the Lagos Railway in Nigeria and also the inventor of a railway braking system? He plainly must have lost out with his patents! More important perhaps, Kendal was reputedly the first to bring a motor car into our village. A nice thought to have a "first" in something!!

Oil 12" x 10". Justin, youngest grandson.

Our house is old and plainly has had a hard life. Its thatched roof, for instance, long gone and replaced with clay pantiles – possibly twice over. The outer walls, originally half-timbered on a brick plinth, now with only odd timbers remaining in the brickwork replacing the timber frame at different times over the centuries. The great Tudor chimney stack still reigns supreme with all four fireplaces revealed and ready to go and one in regular use. The fine Tudor four-centred flat arch fireplace in the Master's Parlour with moulding and panel above hints at finer days, sustained by a minor act of gentrification perhaps, by an early 18th century shell cupboard from elsewhere, installed a bit, as they say in Norfolk, on the "sosh" by reason of a tie-beam having to be hacked into to accommodate it. The stop-ended rafters still carry the original floor boards, some of great width and the saw pit saw marks plain to see. An end wall to a bedroom might just hold the key to even earlier origins. The "expert" revealed to me the "W's" cut into a bressummer to ward off the evil eye, or to keep the Devil at bay, probably the same thing. I can't seem to find them now – perhaps he was pulling my leg! A lean-to studio, rendered over like the rest, deceives superficially, only by reason of its windows. A twist on its roof, made by extending directly from the end hip of the house roof was probably achieved more by accident than design.

By coincidence I was born in just such a house – the walls still rendered over, but in this case the half-timbered frame intact and a similar chimney stack, this one rather more ornate with brick arcading above the string course and thatch.

Our eldest granddaughter has always referred to our home as "a magic house" – it has that feeling. Another member of the family, perhaps with a psychic propensity – aided by the occasional strong smell of shag tobacco emanating always from the same place has suggested the possibility of a ghost albeit a benign one. My wife and I go along with that – the place has the right vibes.

We have three children, six grandchildren and six great grandchildren. Christmas has been a regular family celebration. Christmas dinner, The Queen at three, a musical ensemble of piano, violin, clarinet and recorder. After tea and in the studio a play, full of surprises. Our eldest grandson, staid in childhood and adolescence absolutely hilarious and out-performing the rest.

Home and family will have a dog and we are no exception. Early on a most handsome cocker spaniel puppy became resident. A dog, he really was quite special.

"Out of Lucky Star of Ware, three times champion at Crufts" the record said and I think he knew it. We called him "Tatters". Amiable, always affectionate, he was a perfect companion for the children just out of infancy. To our shame, he only earned his keep once, mating officially with the schoolmaster's bitch resulting in a large and equally handsome litter. Tatters was, however, no respecter of pedigree cocker spaniel bitches. His views were constant and wide-ranging. The gamekeeper seemed ever at odds with him and both made use of various stratagems, the former with really no success and the latter with great cunning and using every ploy under the sun, with even less success. A most effective one was for the ever vigilant Tatters to lay dormant, with one eye cocked, at the top of the stairs leading to the front hall and door. The cue was for a knock at the door followed by its opening in early course. The stairs a straight flight, with possibly fourteen or so risers presented no obstacle, two almighty leaps and Tatters was away. Not necessarily may I say to a distant venue. On the right occasion it could be a lightning strike some three hundred yards up the road where Mrs. Ducker's Border collie bitch had been removed for safe keeping from her kennel to the front bedroom. There was nothing else for it. Tatters would install himself on Mrs. Ducker's back doorstep, raise his head as near as possible to the vertical and howl loudly and without ceasing. As can be imagined, this was extremely trying for Mrs. Ducker and extremely tiring for the eldest of the family one of whom would have to go and fetch him home. Sadly we have never had another dog, but much joy from a succession of bitches and as may be imagined rather less stress. Following on from Tatters, a cocker spaniel bitch, two golden retrievers followed by two Afghan hounds. The latter both rescue dogs

Sophie, the second one was with us to mid-December 2000, and when it happened we knew it would be hard, but nowhere as hard as it turned out to be. For eleven and a quarter years Sophie had been our constant companion and shared our home with us. Not really a "rescue dog" at all she was born the 16th March, 1989. We collected her from the Clipperdown Cottage Kennels at the top of Ringshall Beacon near Dunstable the afternoon of Thursday, August 24th, 1989. With hindsight it would seem the original purchasers of the puppy may never have

Watercolour 7" x 10". "Mixed Doubles".

taken delivery, a fifteen year old arthritic cat was cited as the stumbling block. My diary entry reads: "There at 1 (pm) we liaised with the Southern Area Afghan Rescue and met Sophie five months old. Adorable is the word. T (my wife) absolutely enthralled and home she came with us, back by five (pm)". For much of that first evening, Sophie sat on my lap, facing me, a front paw on each shoulder. It would seem proprietorial rights were in the process of being established, and so it was the start of a love affair between Sophie, ourselves, the children and the grandchildren until, sadly, over eleven years later she had to be put to sleep.

Roguish, infinitely disobedient, so endearing in her mannerisms and demonstrations of affection. At five months a perfect form and stance. The face comical surrounded by a ruff, her head topped by a mass of curls, a kind of immature snub nose, the distinctive "Concorde droop" developing over the months with maturity. So "trying" with her hole scrabbling all over the garden at the time of her so called phantom pregnancies. A charmed life too at odd times as when, for instance she "got out" when staying with us at my eldest son's flat in Bournemouth. Desperately searched by all of us and eventually (it was about half an hour, but seemed like years) traced and caught up with and captured by my wife in the midst of teeming traffic in what can only be described as a miraculous intervention, both of them physically unscathed and Sophie, of course in no way contrite and quite unperturbed by all the fuss.

Retaining many very youthful characteristics, none of us really appreciated that she was, as our veterinary so very kindly put it "Quite an elderly lady". Her passing quiet and dignified the flowers stayed bright in the grass for many weeks thereafter.

Home and family, living in the countryside with mobility paramount, makes it invidious not to mention the motor car. Nowadays regarded as rather a mixed blessing, environmentally flawed, the necessity still endures although much of the real pleasure in the ownership of this mechanical contrivance of whatever quality has now largely gone. Fifty odd years ago, however, should there be a need, one had to try and afford it and having made the acquisition, somehow or other it had to be kept going. Selling and getting back on bike and bus was an option, but rarely implemented. My initial venture was a Triumph Super Seven car of 1930 vintage. It had an all aluminium body already sixteen years old and I was informed it was the first production motor car to be equipped with hydraulic brakes! Not entirely a perfect system. The occasional pumping of the brake pedal if demanded could result in a thin stream of brake fluid emanating from a pinhole in the cap of the master cylinder coming up through a gap in the floor boards towards the driver's face. Not a loss quite to the extent of engine oil burning its way through slack piston rings, but being more expensive, a waste of resources. Tyres of the calibre required were for a time unobtainable. A slit in the side of one became a sewing job covered over on the inside by a patch heavily coated with "Dunlop Rubber Solution". It lasted until the right sized tyres became available. None the less, this little motor gave excellent, if expensive service for some years.

By comparison the next car was quite a sophisticated machine. Yet another Triumph, made in 1934, again with an aluminium body and with a design and style that could hold its own even today. A Triumph Gloria, it was powered by a 9.8 h.p.Coventry Climax long stroke engine above which were mounted large twin carburettors. These both came into operation at around 2,500 r.p.m. (or 45 m.p.h.) with a booming noise that gave an impression of great speed – all very exhilarating. Not yet referred to as "wings" the front mudguards and between these and the bonnet, on cranked stalks, reared two huge chromium plated head lamps. Wire wheels that "groaned" a bit looked racy and the "spare" secured on the outside of the boot lid all added to the car's most graceful lines. A large, lightly spoked steering wheel, wood facia and real leather upholstery made for a smart interior. Once again, however, "pump-up" seats, utilising in each case something like a football bladder only of a different shape. The first Triumph also had them, but of less account apart from comfort, the car being much smaller. A different matter in this second much larger motor. It was important for the seats to be kept well inflated, no latitude for punctures, not even slow ones. For me, being short in stature, this could present problems should one occur when driving, had it not been for the largeness of the steering wheel. This allowed me clear vision of the highway through the spokes should I slowly "descend" to a lower level. However, this would not be apparent to an onlooker and rumour had it that he, or she, had seen Wilson's car go past without a driver!!

I had purchased the car through a garage and had been given to understand that the previous owner was an officer in the RAF. This was borne out for me when I saw a photograph in our local paper in March 1994 of my long departed "Gloria" with owner, taken on a Norfolk airfield.

A sigh perhaps for years past with car ownership now becoming like the mass production process of the car itself and one of stifling intensity that brooks no opposition.

Chapter Ten

CHILDHOOD MEMORY: YARMOUTH AND GORLESTON
_____

My association with Great Yarmouth in general and Gorleston-on-Sea in particular started in the 1920s in a red charabanc – possibly one of Pymer's from Long Stratton tho' I believe his "big bus" was a dark blue – taking us on a day trip to the sea.

Through Acle and along the "straight" (seven miles) I glimpsed with mounting excitement the masts and yards of shipping rising close to and towering high above the Town Hall. A fascination with the sea and ships has always been with me. A visit to other Norfolk sea-sides was not the same. There was the sea and the sand, but not the shipping with the hustle and bustle of commerce that goes with it. The North Quay still had its railway line and one had to look both ways before crossing. The beaches were a joy – so much going on. Great open boats rocking in the surf, all movement as passengers gingerly boarded for a trip out to Scroby Sands. The Revolving Tower dominated the sea-front (the viewing platform revolved at one time, but not the Tower) and commanded the entrance to the Britannia Pier, a fine structure. No less splendid, the Wellington Pier bounded the promenade to the South and behind it was the Nelson Memorial Column. What names to conjure with. The gardens between the piers gave added dignity to the "Front" and were much as they had been for many years, the dress of the promenading older generation harking back to Edwardian times and those of the younger (flapper) set to fashions more than another war away.

The panorama unfolded and the excitement mounted with the customary river trip to Gorleston embarking on a "proper" steamer from the Town Hall Quay. Preferably for me a seat by the engine room hatch to be immersed in the smell of steam and engine oil from contact with hot metal. The engine itself looked huge to my eyes, the movement of piston, crank and prop. shaft of hypnotic fascination. With the quays so full of shipping it was almost a torment to know on what to concentrate one's gaze. This trip of possibly less than two miles, so full of interest that never flagged, seemed over in a trice. Arriving at Gorleston we disembarked by gangway either on to the quay, or, depending on the state of the tide, through a slipway in the quay wall. Here all things were nautical: the great curving sweep of the estuary out to the open sea, the Spending Beach on the other side of the

Oil 16" x 24". A Breezy Day, Gorleston.

Oil 14" x 18". Town Hall Quay, Gt. Yarmouth.

river – for generations a "dry dock" for careening and repairing a multitude of vessels – behind us the tall red bricked harbour light and just ahead the slatted, tapering structure of the Storm House lookout, the drama of whose presence was quite unknown to me at the time. At last to the great Harbour Wall itself, this massive construction of supposedly Dutch origin turning the estuary out to sea and, on the seaward side with its great timbers forming the "Cosies" in whose protection a more perfect way to take the air, canoodle and to sunbathe could surely not be found. Finally and almost at the end, a small, white painted, pagoda like timber building whose use, I must confess, I never discovered.

Gorleston was the place to have a "dip". The wheeled Victorian/Edwardian bathing machines were still there, the wheels awash on a rising tide and towards Hopton the wreck of the steamer beached from the First War accessible to clamber over (a hazardous affair) at really low tides and always the ships, plumes of smoke streaming ahead, or trailing behind, according to the direction and speed of the wind. Countless laden colliers heading South and presumably in ballast when returning North. The harbour in constant use by all kinds of craft, none more impressive than the occasional four masted barque with timber from the Baltic. A paddle steamer clinker built and with tall, thin black and red stack having served for decades as a tug eventually did sea trips. An ancient craft this, dating well back into the 19th century.

Annual holidays at Yarmouth changed to annual holidays at Gorleston. The wheeled rank of bathing machines was replaced by rows of rectangular bleached tents set back from the tideline, but the beach maintained its excellence and the bathing was always safe. Our place to stay moved to a farmhouse down a lane on the outskirts of the town. The farm boasted a 40 acre field (a great size for these parts pre-war) and to this field, coinciding with our holiday, came Sir Alan Cobham's Flying Circus – two or three biplanes at most, providing flights at 3/6d and 7/6d. It was my lucky day. I had a 3/6d ticket and the only other prospective passenger a 7/6d one, so for me too, the longer flight. The plane had two cockpits, my fellow passenger and I sitting in the back one, he behind me, myself grasping a semicircular rail (could it possibly have been a Scarfe Ring mounting for a machine gun) on the fuselage in front of me. The flight was thrilling beyond my wildest dreams, following the river and turning back over Breydon. I don't suppose it lasted ten minutes from start to finish My 3/6d ticket would hardly have got me off the ground!!

The years passed, my father died and my mother continued with holidays at Gorleston, my brother and I joining her occasionally at weekends. Invariably there was an Autumn trip to see the herring fleet in port with boats moored virtually the full width of the river. The tang of salt, the smell of fish, belching smokestacks and a babel of tongues – no wonder that artists growing older became lost in nostalgia.

After the war, holidays were resumed in Gorleston, now with my wife and children. The great surge of 1953 was a catalyst for change. The wreck in its bed

Oil 10" x 12". Walberswick Beach.

Watercolour 7" x 10". "On the Beach", Gorleston.

of shifting sand had long ceased to be within bathing distance. The beach began to disappear revealing ancient groins suggesting a different outlet for the river to the sea and that wonderful timber bastion forming the South side of the harbour entrance gave way to a mixture of steel and concrete, but not before I too had a chance to make my record. Gorleston had long been the haven for a small colony of artists meeting and staying at the White Lion and centred on Campbell Mellon and Rowland Fisher all paying homage to the great Arnesby Brown living a few miles down the road at Haddiscoe and I too fell under that spell.

Now, hurrah, as a result of the extensive sea defences built after the 1953 floods, the beach is again splendid and almost back to what it used to be and any stricture on bathing is not mainly a preoccupation with safety.

Chapter Eleven

A PAINTER IN FRANCE

DIEPPE. To many Dieppe may be seen as a point of departure for more glamorous venues, but to others it can appeal as a microcosm of what is best in France. Architecturally impressive and a cultural centre for the arts in the late 19th and early 20th centuries embracing from Great Britain writers, poets, critics and painters focused on the French painter and Anglophile Jacques-Emile Blanche. Blanche had a house there and a friend in the painter Walter Sickert who also for a time lived just outside Dieppe at Neuville. Walter Sickert in his paintings made familiar such landmarks as the church of St. Jacques, the Cafe des Tribunaux, Statue of Duquesne and the Royal Hotel to mention but four subjects, as well as many other locations, some in quaint corners of the town. Fish restaurants extended to include the adjacent pavements are really quite singular. A Parisian on my right and a Dutchman to the left of me are not just passing travellers, but have made the journey specially for an assignation with the cuisine and are tucking in to enormous platters piled high with fruits of the sea.

In yet another dimension the naval and military actions of 1942 centred on Dieppe, Puy and Pourville tell us the story of immense heroism and of military strategy during this period of the second world war.

West along the coast of Brittany and opposite St. Malo is DINARD. Again the architecture is singular, if in a different vein – more modern, domestic and with possibly an English influence. Part of the town consists of enormous dwelling houses a century or more old and now probably adapted to flats and other conversions. An elderly French lady whose father was a builder told the author these houses catered for wealthy families from across the Channel who came regularly to Dinard for their holidays. One thing she was quite certain about was the one train per family who travelled in the first coach, the servants in the second and the baggage in the third. Not to overlook an artistic connection – Picasso took holidays there and also painted on his visits.

The Department of Finistere has affinities with Cornwall, a coastline to match and artistic traditions that have been instrumental in art movements to modern times. The work of French artists like Millet and Bastien-Lepage influenced

British painters many of whom worked for at least a time in Finistere. Comcarneau was a magnet with its tunny fleet and mosaic pattern of sails.

PONT-AVEN. The school of painting was quite international headed by French artists Paul Gauguin and Emile Bernard. Gauguin's "Yellow Christ" may well be deemed one of the great pictures of the 19th century. The carved subject of the picture hanging in the Chapel at Tremalo on the outskirts of Pont-Aven is redolent of the land, the people and its past. Names associated with the movement like le Bois d'Amour and le Poldu only serve to heighten the atmosphere of the area. Pont-Aven itself remains steeped in the Pont-Aven School and consists mainly of Art Galleries, many showing works in the School's tradition. A prominent member was the Irishman Roderick O'Conor, rather neglected until fairly recent times. A consummate painter of the sea, the Museum at Pont-Aven staged a splendid exhibition of his work in 1984 followed with an exhibition in 1985 by the City of London's Barbican Art Gallery. This exhibition later toured Belfast, Dublin and Manchester. O'Conor's "striped" expressionist landscapes attract great interest. Son of a wealthy and important Irish family O'Conor parallels another artist of note, an English painter, friend of Henri de Toulouse-Lautrec.

PARIS: THE ENGLISHMAN AT THE MOULIN ROUGE. William T. Warrener was the second son of a wealthy and important English family living in the City of Lincoln. He opted for art and distinguished himself at the Art School, Lincoln and the Slade in London before further training in a Paris Atelier and then working in Paris and elsewhere at Grez-sur-Loing like his contemporary O'Conor, possibly mixing to some extent with the American Impressionists. Grez was very popular

Oil 10" x 12". Beach Tents, Dinard.

and quite an international venue. In Paris Warrener got to know Toulouse-Lautrec, maybe moved in the same circle of acquaintances and frequented the fashionable haunts. He is featured in more than one work by Lautrec, but the universal imperishable image of which William Tom Warrener was the subject is the poster of "The Englishman at the Moulin Rouge". Sadly, the "subject" became confused for a time, being attributed to a Mr. W.T.Warner, a theatre impresario, but that error has now been rectified when it was discovered that a preliminary study in the Albi Museum had also been incorrectly attributed. Warrener, unlike O'Conor, was unable to pursue his career as a painter in France. He had to succeed to the family business early and became a pillar of society in the city of his birth and founder of the Lincolnshire Drawing Club, later to become the Lincolnshire Artists' Society.

(The source of information: courtesy of Usher Gallery, Lincoln: William Tom Warrener Exhibition Catalogue, July 13th - September 8th 1974).

COLLIOURE. Having read the biography "The unknown Matisse" by Hilary Spurling, I find myself longing to pay another visit to what I can only describe as "that changeless place".

I enjoyed two painting trips, the first when Rene Pous was still presiding at the Hostellerie des Templier followed by a second some years later when Rene had been succeeded by another member of the family.

Oil 10" x 12". Plage Borema, Collioure.

Friend of the Fauves and a host of School of Paris artists, Rene counted amongst them Picasso, Matisse and the sculptor Maillol to mention but three. The large boat shaped bar of the Templier was lined several deep with pictures by the lesser lights of the school – perhaps they had an "arrangement" with the landlord – the dining and other rooms adorned mainly with works by the great and famous.

What also come to mind is a "wedge" of early photographs of Collioure and its environs blanketed in heavy snow. The date escapes me, but it must have been a highly unusual occurrence and something of a shock to the inhabitants.

The foothills of the Pyrenees embrace Collioure to the North and West, castles and towers abound, including the great Chateau des Templiers within the town. The church tower, at one time serving as a lighthouse and well-placed in that it juts out into the harbour, has been featured by innumerable artists, likewise the brilliantly painted, high prowed boats with the single latecn sail. All redolent of the Moors and the Crusades.

At times, moist air descends from the mountains, the sun filtering through the droplets making for an all enveloping rainbow, and optical delight. Collioure can be magic.

LA ROCHELLE

Marguerite Steen paints a vivid picture albeit a sad one in her book on the artist Sir William Nicholson when they stayed there in the autumn of 1938. The atmosphere seemed clouded by the inevitability of war, full of intrigue and altogether depressing in the extreme. Not that it stopped this great artist from executing the most beautiful work.

The contrast nearly fifty years on could not have been more pronounced. Intensely busy, crowded with townsfolk and with parties of school children on tour with their teachers. The South Basin packed with fishing boats and everywhere alive with the hustle and bustle of commerce. La Rochelle so very interesting historically, quite an artists' paradise and subject wise one could be spoilt for choice. Best just to get one's easel up and in place, or make a start with pencil and pad. The colour was superb. Even our hotel had been adapted from a monastic building with a modern front to a medieval back. An interesting mix repeated for us again a few years later when staying at the Pensione Bucintoro in Venice. Likewise the views from the windows. I could work away from crack of dawn without leaving the room and yet again after supper. At the Pensione, of course, I could even work in bed, looking through a window festooned with geraniums in a three foot thick wall with the prospect of the Salute to feast upon. But I digress. Back to La Rochelle, behind the Grosse Horloge, an arcaded street, the Cathedral and the most wonderful ancient civic buildings. Intimate squares of old and varied dwellings abound, the squares free of traffic and occupied with stalls of every kind. The coast and hinterland too beckoned with a rich variety of incident and landscape. Time was so very much of the essence. Further south at Royan I recalled seeing years past a delicious small oil by the Scottish colourist J.D.Ferguson titled "Twilight Royan" from the collection of Dr. R.A.Lille, OBE. My first introduction to this exciting group of artists and how a selection from the collection ever came to our small Midland town I do not know. It was a generous selection and there was no queue. The Scottish Arts Council had done us proud.

Oil 12" x 16". 'Mistral', Bay of Cannes.

CANNES. Chemin du Piccoloret it said, about six feet wide, climbing in a winding fashion to the top of the escarpment with a gradient that seemed about 1:2. Off to one side and near the top was the Villa. I may have made comments elsewhere on these, but this was the goods. Spacious, some floors with a mosaic finish, a terrace with balustrade and a prospect with Cannes extending to the Golf de Napoule and the Ile St. Marguerite. To the South West the Esterel Mountains. In front and below the terrace the ground falling away at an alarming angle with ancient olive trees teetering in eroding soil to dwellings feet below. To the East winding lanes through the remnants of old olive groves and other trees led to Le Cannet, the Avenue Victoria and the Villa de Bosquet, home of Pierre Bonnard and his wife Marthe from 1926 where he spent much of every year until his death in 1947, and thereafter held in sequestration for many years. Not much of a villa by all accounts considering the stature of the artist, but the house, gardens and environs probably finite and without limitation to his genius. No instant frames for this man, just cut a piece of canvas from the roll, pin it to the wall and paint. Always seeing, always creating. Entrancing to the viewer and none more so than the host of little drawings in the Exhibition promoted by the Art Council in 1984, starting in Nottingham and continuing to other venues, including Norwich. For many, including myself, this exhibition gave a breathtaking insight into the world of the painter. The catalogue remains with me, a treasured possession.

And what of the painting trip? As always in a warm clime, drawing, painting and swimming, generally in that order and for days a searing blast claimed to be the Mistral, but to my mind emanating from the Sahara. Eyes full of grit, skin smarting from a whiplash of sand blown horizontally at gale force. It was hot and perseverance brought results, but the human interest element was somewhat thin on the ground. A full scale reproduction of a Spanish galleon provided the motif for a change of subject. I marvelled at the hugeness of the timbers used in the construction. Instant relief from the wind by travelling inland to Grasse and Vence.

We left, I felt too soon, but all had been arranged. The coast road beckoned with a stop at Antheor of the red rocks and a stay just west of St. Tropez. I changed to working in water colour. A feast of multicoloured sails at Cavalaire and then inland. West of Aix and on to Le Baux, and a tiny painting in my studio reminds me of a similar painting trip made years previously. An idyllic lodging, early morning on the terrace charmed by the song of nightingales. My friend Stanley, a hat with vast brim flapping and sandals flopping, striding forth with his water colours. The prospect to Le Baux an ageless place with Moorish ruins, a medieval village, high on a rock outcrop and views south over fields of lavender, sunflowers and distant olive groves. Not so far away, Nimes from across a plain of olives an atmospheric wonder and what of Nimes itself; the bottle green waters of the Quai del la Fontaine, the perfection of the Maison Carree. Blood in the sand of the amphitheatre still in use. Another time with sketchbook in hand a walk along the top of the Pont du Gard. All this around and about. Setting up my easel for a small painting of Alphonse Daudet's Mill outside the little town of Fontveille with its numerous "cut out" sheet metal signs in black. Always space, plenty of space, except at Arles when our first visit coincided with a festival and a vast concourse of gypsies and horses from the Camargue. One can well understand why this land so captivated the sculptor and painter John Skeaping. In Arles I looked for the house where Vincent Van Gogh, in great distress, cut off his ear. I pondered how this genius, having spent a lifetime from painting potato gatherers and similar on his native heath to slaving away in the Midi had never sold a picture and probably never would have if brother Theo hadn't been in the business in Paris. Who could argue that Gauguin should not have gone to the South Seas? Staying would not have produced the masterpieces he sent back from those faraway places.

GREZ AND MORET-SUR-LOING. Returning from painting near Bandol there was a pilgrimage we were determined to make. Leaving the motorway we took the

Tourist Route and headed for Grez, home to Frederick Delius the English composer of German descent who moved in 1897 and lived here, except for one brief period, until his death in 1934. Fortuitously we met the Mayor who took us straight to the spot, a small bridge I had seen reproduced in many paintings. Shades of those 19th century artists from Europe and America who made it their home for a while and a reminder of W.T. Warrener from Lincoln and that little gem of a snow picture that must have been painted close by, acquired and now hanging in the Usher Gallery. Time was precious, no chance to paint and we moved on to Moret and to Alfred Sisley, booking in at the Black Horse. A quick drive round to St. Mammes and the purchase of a book not only providing small reproductions of each of his pictures painted locally, but also a map, with each one numbered and an illustrated tour was ready made. Moret, a fortified town and how little it appeared to have changed, not even the course of the effluent into the river! Nor the Poplars, though of another generation. We visited Sisley's house and then his grave marked with a vast, sombre lump of rock so much in contrast to the joy and sunshine expressed in his pictures. Next a furious onslaught with my 5"x7" sketch pad and a small box of water colours. Working was difficult, I had to stand. Supper was memorable, the rarest of rare steaks I have ever consumed, then retirement to a most comfortable bed. Next day more to see as we headed for the ferry, Fontainbleu and Barbizon. From Sisley back to Corot and Daubigny!! The date: 16.6.90. The final note in my diary "A marvellous journey, an all round lovely trip".

Chapter Twelve

AN ITALIAN EXPERIENCE

On reaching the border crossing into Italy we stopped, I looked back and executed a small watercolour of Menton extending up from the coastal plain into the foothills towards Sospel indelibly printed in my memory of a painting by the artist Bertram Nicholls. As I worked I felt there could scarcely be a prospect more wonderful, or colour more exhilarating. Comparisons, odious or not, didn't really come into it. As we journeyed on along the Italian Riviera "first time" impressions registered to surpass the one seen previously. Reaching Genoa and passing on the seaward side by successive bridges over numerous inlets and ravines, all seen through a misty golden light, the dreamlike quality of the landscape continued. An intermittent plunge from darkness into light as lengths of tunnel continuously gave way to lengths of highway in brilliant sunshine had me marvelling at what must be an engineering triumph of motorway construction. Porto Fino mentioned elsewhere seems to have been completely missed likewise La Spezia. On to Lerici and a thought crosses my mind on the sad demise by drowning of the poet Shelley. Within a trice we are at our destination, Tellaro, which immediately promised to be a location par excellence for anyone with artistic leanings. My elder son had joined us for this trip and shared the driving. All three of us could be "free spirits". I have mentioned elsewhere the "Shrine", which was the subject for a painting. The tiny harbour, reached by a tortuous path was entrancing and invariably peopled by children fishing. On another occasion, besieged by tumultuous waves in a storm of great ferocity it seemed that the harbour and dwellings huddled around it would be completely overwhelmed and thus it must have seemed and been for hundreds of years.

Pisa and Florence beckoned. A signpost to Carrara away off the coast road recalled images old and yet to be seen. The gift of a bunch of flowers from an extended arm as we made the ascent warmed the heart and language limitations had no meaning.

Marble surfaces, polished by a thousand feet gave pause for thought that within a few days the leaning tower would be indefinitely closed to visitors for the "lean" to be stabilised. At the time of writing I think this has now been accomplished and reflections on these polished surfaces will be renewed. What

Watercolour 7" x 10". Evening, Gulf of Spezia.

Oil 16" x 20". Anglers, Tellaro.

can I say of Florence. Volumes could be written to say but half. Plunging into a maelstrom of traffic, determined not to show a trace of nerve, a pleasant disembodied voice at my steering elbow asked "Are you looking for a park?" From the corner of my eye I saw a red sports car had come alongside. Not being my best in surreal situations and deeming it prudent not to take my eyes off the cars ahead I hastily muttered loudly in the affirmative. The voice came back "I'll draw ahead, follow me". End of problem. The Good Samaritan was a young Danish business executive. It's a small world and not necessarily that surreal.

Oil 9" x 12". Gulf of Spezia.

Switching from drawing in watercolour to painting in oil and vice versa can perhaps be a bit like having a swop in writing from one hand to the other – at least when one is working en plein air. Best to have a spell with one before changing, or the muse departs!! I can say I wasn't "afflicted" whilst at Tellaro and if the reader is "of the persuasion" he might care to make a visit, if he hasn't already done so. The kippers supplied by the greengrocer were boxed in Great Yarmouth.

Chapter Thirteen

THE VENICE EXPERIENCE

Venice defies description, all superlatives are an understatement and anything one says really falls short of the reality. In fact, it is a presumption to even attempt it. An old artist once said to me "Where there is water there is beauty" and that is a truism if ever there was one. A thousand years of splendour coalesce in the slip slap of water against the steps of the Grand Canal, rocking the gondolas tied to their candy striped mooring posts and reflecting the superb churches, ducal palaces, great houses and the innumerable bridges in the unbelievable unity which is Venice.

The absence of motorised road traffic heightens the perceptions and one's vision becomes more acute. Water bubbling up noisily through apertures in manhole covers spreads across St. Mark's Square – Venice in Peril perhaps – but so it has been throughout the centuries. The Campanile impresses, but tends to block the view. The superb facade of the Basilica holds us transfixed, replete with refurbished lions, the gold leaf appliqué glittering in the sun. The interior a feast of marble and mosaics. The wing flapping furore of countless pigeons criss-crossing over the square. In the background, harmonising all, the strains of a Viennese waltz from the string quartet playing with great fluency behind the arcading of a restaurant. Then a change of tempo, determined not to be boring by repetition and with great gusto launching off into a foot tapping hit of the day – "Start spreadin the news – I'm leaving today – I wanna be part of it – New Y New Y... and never mind, there is no soloist anyway and it's the tune that gets you, not the lyric and for us it's Venice, Venice all the way.

The Via Garibaldi on a Sunday morning, the Via is partly superfluous as there is no traffic, just people. The Venetians are out and about, the prospect up the street to the Maria della Salute and I would like to use the word divine, but must not any more than intimating horror when "sounding off" about the Bridge of Sighs. A huge vessel floats in and moors adjacent to the Riva degli Schiavoni blocking any view of the Isola di St. Georgio and the great church rising above it. These great churches of wondrous design and packed with artefacts are legion and can so easily be placed and named from an infinite range of guide books and need no repetition here. Very early a.m. and later p.m. are the painters' times of day and visiting times for religious houses close at 12 noon. The Accademia must not be missed, nor should

Oil 12" x 10". Entrance to the Piazzetta, di St. Marco, Venice.

Oil 12" x 10". The Vin Garibaldi, Venice.

the Scuola Dalmata of St. George and St. Trypone. John Ruskin is a man to read and nearer our time John Singer Sargent a painter to look at.

Monet and J.M.W. Turner continue to delight. Amongst the immortals Bellini, Titian, Tintoretto and Veronese sit astride the 15th and 16th centuries, the baroque creation of the Salute by Longhena in the 17th century, already mentioned, is spearheaded by the Dogana, seat of Customs. Into the 18th century Canaletto continues to amaze with his precision of detail and Francesco Guardi with his silvery architectural evocations. All to be immediately recognised were the masterpieces painted but yesterday. The Peggy Guggenheim Gallery, not far

Oil 12" x 10". Statue Vittorio Emanuelle The Riva Schiavoni, Venice.

distant, will keep us up to date with modern trends. A banner elsewhere in town loudly proclaims in great red letters FUTURISMO & FUTURISMI, an Exhibition I never got to see. In the eighteenth century Tiepolo continued the high artistic tradition of his earlier forbears in churches, the Accademia and elsewhere. On the Riva Schiavoni the equestrian statue of Vittorio Emmanuelle with raised sabre commands our attention and around the plinth and detailed relief, dozens of "Venice Cats" have long had their home. The mighty equestrian statue of Bartolommeo Colleoni intimidates with its fierceness in a Square with the same name as an adjacent church. Narrow thoroughfares sometimes packed and sometimes void of tourists in holiday attire highlight, somewhat incongruously, the odd, smart suited and tied Venetian businessman replete with briefcase and rolled umbrella. Venetian weather can be a mixed bag.

The islands must not be missed. Furthest out, Torcello is historically the ancient of ancients. Next in, Burano, famed for its exquisite lace making is for me a painter's paradise. What blissful hours I have spent along the canals from a kaleidoscopic joy of light and shade in the town to opalescent transparencies of sea and sky looking out across the lagoon to the shadowy hues of the Venice skyline. Closer to Venice the island of Murano, its glass making so long famed and a glory in itself. "Nearest home" the island of San Michele with a church and a large cemetery not normally visited.

A journey by rail takes some beating and having drawn into the station, a speedy transfer to a motor launch and a two mile extravaganza along the Grand Canal to one's hotel or pensione just sets the seal for a painting trip in excelsis.

Watercolour 7" x 10". The Lagoon, Venice.

Chapter Fourteen

ON CRUISING – JUST A NOTE

A dozen reasons against, most of them valid, crowd in on any contemplation to indulge. Being cosseted around the clock for even a few days is not to be ignored, and providing the ship is right all else may well fall into place. Destinations are legion, some like it hot – around the Med for instance and some like it cold and the rigours of the North Cape could be tempting. Joining the ship in far distant waters to even hotter and more exotic climes may take precedence. We chose the first and, on boarding, were to be paged by the Purser. The "emergency" was at its height and my old pony-hide case with my paints, well strapped, but not locked, was under suspicion, soon sorted. Ships of all kinds have been a passion and a preliminary exploration of cabin and decks exciting. Two sittings for supper, we opted for the later one. Our table for six all carefully thought out. Janey and Richard a young married couple, Pauline on her own, my wife Thirza and I, the five of us to be joined by one of the ship's officers. Generally amongst the first to be seated and amongst the last to leave, and thus it continued throughout the cruise. In the interim, delightful and stimulating conversation with much banter and hilarity. The ship's owner had some of his extensive art collection tastefully hung and displayed throughout the vessel, good for the digestion. Then to the evening's entertainment with an extensive and talented cast including a member of minute dimensions to whom we attached the name of "Pork Chop", quite a star of the show.

Dancing was a must and no one more versatile and fluent than the ship's doctor. A second night had seen queasy stomachs with the Bay of Biscay running true to form, but no one succumbed. By early light our first port of call, Portimao in the Algarve. Time for me to execute a watercolour and to take advantage of the light. Yesterday a small oil marine of a grand sea and sky had the cruise liner Canberra (much faster) as a feature passing us on its way to the Canary Islands. A pleasant day ashore and an art gallery of some distinction owned and manned by a fellow countryman had me wondering why I had never thought up a similar idea. At sea again and we had to heave-to for, sadly, an ill passenger to be put ashore at Cadiz. Shuffle board and other deck games to the fore. All rather trite, but stimulating to the point of a constant endeavour to excel. With hindsight,

Oil 10" x 12". Harbour Prospect, La Rochelle.

Oil 10" x 12". Gathering Storm, St. Tropez.

generating a degree of interest out of all proportion, but that's what successful cruising is about. Likewise the attendant crew from the Philippines. Pat, our waiter, courteous and efficient, easy in his manner and utterly devoid of servility. I understand he is now Commissioned. The girls, petite and pretty charmed everyone without exception. Always around, but never obtrusive. Our next call at Barcelona and a long stay on shore with so much to see, not least the great Olympic Stadium nearing completion. Antoni Gaudi's architectural and still incomplete wonder the Sagrada Familia Cathedral and many other buildings by the same hand.

The evening meals continued in their variety and joyous social fraternity, cabaret to be watched or deserted for the gaming tables and always, with infectious enthusiasm, the dancing. The greatest fun and not a moment in which to be bored. If this was hedonism, we had missed out to date and now surely a chance to make up for lost time. A small watercolour of the city harbour entrance and skyline was all I managed to accomplish here, but it still "rings a bell" when leafing through my sketch book.

More painting on board. A suggestion I might like to contemplate an engagement of Artist in Residence didn't take long to discard. The unadulterated enjoyment of this brief interlude was not to be tampered with, or any tremor likely to disturb the flowing pattern of sociability we now enjoyed.

Heading for the French Riviera, the weather changed with a wild sky and strong wind whipping up the waves as we anchored off St. Tropez. Away on the first tender out we headed straight down the quay to the Museum and art gallery visited on previous occasions. Still "fresh" and exciting and full of the old favourites: Matisse, Bonnard, Signac, Marquet and a number of lesser lights. A "must" in the first instance as, true to form, the gallery closed at 12 noon. A furious sky pre-empted the coming storm, but I set up my easel and made a start with continual flashes of lightning and thunder claps heralding worse to come. However, I made good progress before the heavens opened and we were finally engulfed. Shelter was out of the question and like drowned rats we headed for the tender, each of us virtually awash. A hot shower and a good lunch did much to restore our equilibrium and then back to the tender again during a brief respite, but to resume our trip was not to be. The storm returned with a vengeance and did not abate until late in the afternoon. Early evening I painted from the fore peak of the vessel, St. Tropez having regained its usual composure with a superb evening light and a quietening sea. We weighed anchor around 9 pm. A brilliant sun greeted us early in the morning as we sailed to Menorca and anchored in the great harbour of the capital Mahon for so long associated with the British Navy. A tour of the island in the morning enabled me to work in water colour and during the afternoon, also in oil from the quay side enhanced by children playing and a large yacht preparing to sail to Sardinia. Next day to Ibiza and to the capital with the same name. Another dockside painting with the motif of ancient buildings and the cathedral outlined high above on the escarpment. Yet another adjustment of my watch to take account of a change of time relevant to our next destination. Evenings continued with a social rapport unabated. Leo, our sixth at table so extremely knowledgeable and such a charming host when entertaining us to cocktails in his cabin before dinner. Near two days at sea this time and with Gibraltar to starboard we rapidly approached Morocco, made landfall and docked in Tangier. A different world this, the old town below the new one. Into the Casbah, shops with carpets of every description, brass, copper and silver ware in the greatest profusion and wonderfully worked leather goods pressed on us from all sides with cheeky urchins adding to the general confusion arising from haggling. No alternative but to present like with like – the tourists in their shorts, the Moroccans in their djellabas and ornate leather slippers, all for us rather suggestive of Arabian Nights. The mixture of throbbing drums and wailing pipes followed us into the souks. Market traders sitting, or standing with their wares around them and snake charmers and other entertainers fascinated us, besieged as we were by constant deals and hard-pressed bargains. Glistening white castellated walls and buildings all around, a sky of brilliant blue, one calls to mind that Tangier is not infrequently referred to as "a jewel", the atmosphere so infectious with little chance to stop and reason, or really the desire to do so. Refreshed in a palatial apartment with quantities of mint tea slowly we found our way back to the ship, a few laden with their purchases, the majority with arrangements for these to "follow on".

Oil 10" x 12". Siesta Time, Mahon.

However, no rest for the painter. Everything now ready made and just to be "sorted". The quay side in the afternoon alive with the occupants of the Casbah from the morning. A back cloth of sea, sand hills and the oh so brilliant sky. Those wonderful hats and decorated leather slippers now enhanced by coats and jackets of every colour merging with bolts of fabric and the usual stock of carpets. Pencil, water colours and oil paints all pressed into service.

An extensive journey out into the hinterland made the visit to Tangier even more memorable, the poverty of the countryside contrasting with the opulence of dwellings owned by westerners from Europe and America. Socialites, statesmen and writers et al have lived and visited in great numbers. A shadier side has been well documented in publications over the years.

At sea again and a dense fog reminds me we are heading north as reaching Oporto after a rough night at sea we have to heave-to before entering the harbour. The fog soon departs and an interesting itinerary lies ahead. We stifle a great desire to tour the city and choose the Portuguese landscape instead. A 15th century palace, a 12th century castle followed by a visit to a most impressive shrine. I really don't know how we fitted it all in, with time to do two slight water colours in my small sketch book. Thank goodness for thick cartridge paper that doesn't buckle. We spent what little was left of the rest of the day on board and I managed a small oil of the docks. After the fog, the light was quite special. The Portuguese landscape most impressive, well wooded on rounded hills, lots of great

Oil 10" x 12". On The Quay, Tangier.

eucalyptus trees. Our usual evening in the most excellent company we have enjoyed throughout and absolutely no abatement in our enthusiasms. Travelling home the Bay of Biscay was at its kindest. I note in my diary that I played three good games of shuffle board with "Joe". Anyway, I think they must have been good, I see I added the rider "and won all three". Packing and saying farewells to the many friends particularly those who shared our table. We saw them all again, some staying with us here and later joining us on a cruise to a colder clime, but that's another story. I have a small water colour study of the Needles made on the outward journey, a nice reminder of a really great time.

Chapter Fifteen

ON TREES AND WOODS

We all get pleasure from trees and woods and country folk are particularly well blessed in this respect. Whether in hedgerow or forest, the impact on the senses can be marked. We in this part of the country have a wide variety of hardwoods to see and many in woodlands with an understorey of coppice. The tall, clean stems of the "standards" bear witness to a best financial return on the tree reaching maturity and a benefit arising from game conservation should not be ignored. A two storey tree crop can have its limitations. The mighty oak, perhaps at its best with 150 to 200 years of growth can be perfection in its use and permanence. A twist of fate that the "queen" of the forest may be a turkey (oak), by far the least durable and least valuable of the species. A form of incipient decay with the timber still sound, can produce a rich, dark colour unmatched for period furniture and seldom matched for value. The sweet chestnut can run the oak a close second and being much quicker to cure when cut and "kinder" to work may well be favoured with very old house restoration so much in vogue. The timber merchant will shake his head gloomily and mutter "look out for shakes". However, these can affect all trees although I must confess sweet chestnut has a risk in this regard.

We are all familiar with the couplet on leafing "When the oak's before the ash we can all expect a splash; but when the ash is before the oak we can then expect a soak". Perhaps there may be something in it? The ash became universally renowned in the construction of that most durable of fighter bombers, the Mosquito and in any case has always been the wood from which best tool handles are made. Beech is much used in the making of upholstered furniture and may well be considered superior to birch, which can be cheaper and perhaps more plentiful. The sycamore, such a lovely tree and highly valued for its timber when it has a patination referred to as "lace grained" generally confined to the first few feet of the bole. Likewise the walnut, not so often seen in woodlands and again of great value when well figured and consequently highly prized by the producers of veneers. Out of woodlands and into specialist plantations, the growing of cricket bat willows requires no explanation. Until recently likewise the hybrid poplar grown entirely for match production, but now I suspect a use of declining interest.

Moving into what are generally known as soft hardwoods because of their uses in turnery and mainly a pole crop are the alders. Both the rough and smooth barked varieties, grown in damp locations and until recently used by the brush manufacturers for brush backs and handles. Employing hundreds in factories, this could still be called a rural industry. I fear a new industry has dawned of plastic and nylon!! The underwood (or coppice) use has at least survived in part. In the south mainly sweet chestnut and in these parts mainly hazel. A hazel "broach" is doubtless still in great demand by house thatchers to secure the reed or wheat straw covering to roofs. No longer sought by agricultural suppliers to thatch wheat and barley stacks. The combine reigns supreme. And what to do with the tops cut off from the rod? At one time sold in bundles by the 1000 for fire lighting, for pea sticks and so on. Also to bewail the loss of chimneys in new house construction and declaim that nuclear fission is not the answer. But let's get back to trees and woods. The lime as a standard, or pollarded, has a timber not dissimilar to alder. It is sometimes referred to as "bass". At the other end of the spectrum is hornbeam. A smallish tree the timber of which is so intensely hard that over generations it has been used for cogwheels, or at least the cogs in wind and waterwheel machinery.

The solid YEW of ancient origin still "stands guard" around most churchyards and in a corner of old farmhouse gardens. When of reasonable size and not too "fluted" it is ideal for the carvers' art and superior furniture. Remiss of me for not having so far mentioned the ELM. How far "the mighty has fallen" because of Dutch elm disease. These most graceful of trees will revive. Elm seem much liked by the French for furniture. Perhaps I shouldn't mention in the same context that it gets "the worm"!! When speaking of "drains" I failed to mention "Trunks" which are oblong boxes, open ended, about 15 inches square made of massive elm planks. These are let into dykes at strategic points, splayed and side-railed to provide crossing places for stock. Elm lasts in these conditions. Heavy machinery should stay away otherwise the "trunk" descends to a level lower than the drain it serves and foundation ballast is seldom the answer.

So many other hardwoods to mention. The willow with "withies" from lop or top for many uses not least, and now also gone, for herring swills made in Great Yarmouth until a few years ago. Heavy enough when filled with logs!! Birch "lop and top" for the steeple chase jumps. The great black poplar can be an immense tree. Perhaps 100 feet high and just as wide, its deeply fissured bark quite unmistakable. The aspen poplar with its "shivering" silver leaves tends to make one feel cool even on a hot summer day.

And so to the softwoods. Scots Pine. Our only indigenous one with us through the ages as a structural timber particularly in house roofs. Carcasses for fine furniture to be adorned with mahogany and even more exotic veneers. LARCH which sheds its needles in the winter and can be a most durable and quality timber if well grown, really has to come from the west for the benefit of a higher rainfall. Boat skins are a premium use, possibly to be cladded over and the

European variety seems to be superior to the Japanese by virtue of its habit of growth. Douglas fir, Sitka spruce and the reader will be saying what about the Lawson cypress, Norway spruce and great redwoods *et al* and don't forget the *Thuja plicata!!*

The Tree and products from it continue to serve us all despite alternatives and advances in modern technology. Sometimes, it is difficult to relate the product back to the timber from which it is derived. Worth a thought perhaps and maybe to even go a stage further to try and visualise the tree itself, which, before conversion is such an influence on our lives in general and on the environment in particular.

Chapter Sixteen

ON AGRICULTURE

Earliest memories as a small boy living in the country are of large machines introduced to bring back into cultivation the areas of heavy clay land which had gone out of production in the nineteen twenties. A cyclical depression had once again hit the agricultural industry and by the early nineteen thirties there were signs of a return to some kind of prosperity. The Gyrotiller, possibly a North American import was a large self propelled cultivator, the huge tines circular mounted at the rear of the machine rotated deeply into the earth as the machine moved forwards loosening roots and breaking up the "sod". First, of course, the thorn bushes, which had usually become rife and infested the fields, would have to be cleared and burnt and all overgrown hedges cut back and trimmed to their rightful proportions. Following the Gyrotiller were the steam ploughs – bigger than the average traction engine – operating at each end of a field and each with an endless hawser pulling a set of ploughshares to a depth of several inches. Great stuff for small boys on their bikes to trace the whereabouts of these monsters and to watch the work in progress. I have mentioned under "Boundaries and Drains" the procedures which were part and parcel of the process.

From somewhere fixed in my mind at this time was the mantra that Britain, relying on its own resources, produced only sufficient food to last its population a matter of months. A belief I don't think I really discarded until a few years prior to my retirement!

Post-war it was all systems go. Farming profitability maintained, virtually all land was in production. Landowners and farmers in the van, vied with one another to produce heavier yielding crops and ever finer stock. A 1½ tons per acre of good malting barley in 1946 had been virtually doubled in yield by different varieties in the next thirty years. It became difficult to stay abreast with new and improved strains of seed coming on the market. The name Nickerson's may still be a byword!

The full backing of science and chemistry, channelled through the vast resources of huge industrial conglomerates marketed herbicides and pesticides, good, bad and indifferent, for every appropriate ill. Some lasted only a very few years before being withdrawn from the market, but wild life suffered.

Oil 9" x 12". Ploughing at Hales (young horse in trace).

Oil 9" x 12". Sheep in the Snow, Haddiscoe.

Machines of all kinds grew bigger from prairie style combines for corn harvesting to luxury milking parlours, circular, in tandem, or abreast, which could, if required, play tunes to encourage cows to drop their milk readily, increase yields and to keep them all happy and in good heart. Failing that, a veterinary service on hand to advise, with a training taking many years to complete.

As the machinery grew larger, the farms grew bigger and the labour force smaller, albeit with possibly a greater degree of expertise in some aspects than could be obtained in the past. A dozen men hoeing (singling) the sugar beet seedlings has long given way to an individual seed encapsulated in its own cocoon and gently inserted into the seed bed by a machine of some complexity, at a proper interval to reach maturity without further disturbance. The equally laborious task of hand-pulling wild oats from a cereal crop may well be carried out by a tractor with clearance, spraying the offending weed just prior to the crop reaching maturity. Here again, progress goes on apace and this by now may well be "old hat".

At the time of writing (April 2001) I cannot recall a more complete misery to be endured by the farming community and a host of others than the present Foot and Mouth epidemic. Doubtless it will pass and we must hope, with lessons to be learned on containment and perhaps even, eventual eradication.

Oil 20" x 24". The Wheatfield, Raveningham,

Chapter Seventeen

THE SEA

Most of my painting time has been spent in East Anglia and much of it in the locality of our home in Norfolk some five miles from the boundary with East Suffolk. Earlier I worked in the West Country and latterly in Dorset. My last painting excursion to Cornwall was at the time of our fiftieth wedding anniversary and for my wife to visit her oldest friend living at Pendeen near Lands End. En route we stayed at Bideford and all the excitement of previous visits to Devon and Cornwall returned. A chance to work again at The Burrows with the prospect of Appledore before me followed by a study of shoreline and cliffs at Westward Ho. The following day to Saunton Sands and a shoreline with incomparable sea and sky remembered from years past and now the subject of yet another painting. On to Newquay calling to mind a big sea off Pentire point in the winter of 1983 and to look up friends retired from Nottinghamshire.

With the weather steadily deteriorating, a final "leg" to Penzance and the Queen's Hotel coinciding with a deluge and a near hurricane. I had to work from our bedroom window looking East to St. Michael's Mount, virtually invisible with the sea in ferment and the road along the "prom" awash and only occasionally glimpsed through the scud and spray. The Hotel, despite the passage of years, still with the memories of Sir A.J. Munnings, the fraternities at Newlyn, St. Ives and the villages around.

The fascination with the sea in storm is inexorably compelling and for me it has always been so. A few years ago, very early in the morning I was sheltering at the foot of the cliffs in Gorleston. The prospect was absolutely awe inspiring with the piers to the harbour entrance only visible as intermittent thin dark lines. At the far end, appearing little more than a large buoy, the coastguard lookout. The Gorleston breakwater was marked by crashing breakers exploding thunderously against the unseen concrete resulting in huge plumes of spray thrown high against the leaden sky. The beach itself completely engulfed with the aftermath of the storm's fury and the promenade awash with floating debris to the foot of the cliff. I had my paints – brought with some heart searching – and got to work. How glad that I could. Such occurrences on this scale are not frequent and the opportunity seldom occurs. More recently still and a chance to paint from the

Watercolour 7" x 10". Regatta, Poole Harbour.

Oil 16" x 20". The Trawl Basin, Lowestoft. (RBA Winter Exh. 1967. Cat. No 386.)

Southwold side of the harbour entrance. A rare light and a truly splendid sea with an endless stretch of breakers, no apparent troughs between, piled high and reaching back to the horizon. A sizeable vessel a mile or so off, only the superstructure seen with the occasional glimpse of the hull.

We read that J.M.W. Turner had himself lashed to the mast in order to draw when crossing a turbulent Channel. His genius was far reaching and yet he still believed in a search for that element of truth.

A purely marine subject does not, in essence, have to conform to either an abstract, or figurative interpretation and it is only by the addition of figures, shipping, or similar, that the character of the composition is changed. Sky and sea uninhibited allows the mind to travel freely in conjecture and for the senses to have a field day. No wonder that as a subject it charms millions. Subconsciously the viewer can move from one 'ism to another quite smoothly without any cultural hiccups – J.M.W. Turner to Joan Eardley for instance. Conversely, a Mary Potter back to a Turner watercolour beginning – schools of painting within the genre blending effortlessly. Include a boat and "the case is altered" except perhaps in the hands of a consummate master and these are rather thin on the ground!!

The introduction of a motif such as a four master under full sail, large in the frame, in the right hands, can have a terrific visual impact and who wouldn't fall for a Montague Dawson et al given the opportunity. The sea, the sea, without such a motif, at auction at any rate, however good, unlikely to reach the same financial heights. Perhaps a collector should be a little bit more discerning. I can recall a sea piece by Sir William Llewellyn, a not particularly well known PPRA, that elevated him in my books anyway to a stature far and away above the one he normally seems to enjoy. What a bridge this genre can provide for the student in art history. The sea, wedded to an infinity of sky can only be a catalyst for unity and beauty whether drawn from the North Sea, the Bay of Biscay, the arctic, or the tropics. Drawn from the raging fury of a great storm it must surely transcend towards the sublime.

BIOGRAPHICAL NOTE

Geoffrey William Wilson, born Norfolk 1920. Working from 1953 following contact with near neighbour Sir John Arnesby Brown, RA. Studied under and worked closely with marine artist Rowland Fisher, ROI., RSMA., from 1956 to 1963 and also much helped by Anna Airy, ROI., RE., during the latter part of that period.

Exhibited at the Royal Academy, the Paris Salon, The Royal Institute of Oil Painters for over twenty years to 1979 (some fifty works) and, on sending, to the Royal British Artists and the Royal Society of Marine Artists. Work also shown in the travelling exhibitions of the Art Bureau.

Major one man exhibitions at Great Yarmouth 1962/3, Scunthorpe 1964 and at Lincoln in 1967 having moved to Lincolnshire in 1963. Shared exhibitions in York 1979 and 1980.

Represented in public collections at Great Yarmouth, Lincoln and Plymouth, Mass.

Retired as a Chartered Surveyor to his house at Thurlton, Norfolk in January 1983 to paint full-time, working extensively in East Anglia and Dorset as well as abroad – mainly in France and Italy. During this period he had exhibitions in Windsor, Lavenham, London, Bournemouth and in Norfolk. A shared exhibition at East Bergholt in 1999.

A past President of the Lincolnshire Artists' Society.

ACKNOWLEDGEMENTS

My best thanks to the staff at the Reference Department, Great Yarmouth Central Library who answered my questions on the Revolving Tower, other landmarks and on the wreck off Gorleston beach.

To the members of staff at Easton who kindly listened to and endorsed a paragraph on my chapter Boundaries and Drains. To Michael Parkin and Ian Collins for their very helpful comments, and to 'Reflections' of Norwich for the transparencies.

My most grateful thanks must go to our Nephew Ted Mawby, a retired librarian, for converting all my pages on his state of the art computer set-up. To Xenia his wife for proof reading the text and for her usual grace and charm in response to my frequent telephone intrusions over the past year into the otherwise even tenor of their lives.

Finally, of course, to my dear wife for her constant support, not only given over this book, but throughout our many happy years together.

GW